TIME'S UP!

Understanding and Preventing Workplace Harassment

PAULA J. RICCI

www.hrcoachusa.com

Table of Contents

INTRODUCTION 5
- THE WORLD WE LIVE IN 5
- #METOO/TIME'S UP 6
- HARASSMENT AND THE BOTTOM LINE 8
- WHY EMPLOYEES SUE 9

CHAPTER 1 11
- DISCRIMINATION DEFINED 11
- HARASSMENT DEFINED 13
- TYPES OF HARASSMENT 14

CHAPTER 2 24
- CULTURE AND LEADERSHIP 24
- THE BYSTANDER EFFECT 26
- COMMIT TO REAL CHANGE 28
- SUPERVISOR'S ROLE - T.I.M.E 29

CHAPTER 3 31
- BENEFITS OF HAVING AN EFFECTIVE POLICY 31
- ELEMENTS OF AN EFFECTIVE POLICY 32
- COMMUNICATING THE POLICY 35

CHAPTER 4 36
- BENEFITS OF TRAINING 36
- RESISTANCE 37
- SUPERVISOR VS EMPLOYEE TRAINING 37
- HOW TO CONDUCT TRAINING 39

CHAPTER 5 ....**41**

    RECEIVING THE COMPLAINT 41

    GATHERING INFORMATION 42

    CONDUCTING THE INVESTIGATION...43

    COMPLETING YOUR INVESTIGATION 44

    TAKING ACTION/COMMUNICATION 45

CHAPTER 6 ....**48**

    ELEMENTS OF GOOD DOCUMENTATION 48

    MANAGING DOCUMENTATION..50

Why Now?

Introduction

THE WORLD WE LIVE IN

You can't turn on the news or flip through your daily alerts without hearing or reading about a new claim against a celebrity, producer, newsperson, politician or executive. Make no mistake, the time has come when people are standing up to harassers with their complaints, concerns and allegations. These recent allegations, lawsuits and firings are empowering people to speak out and share their stories. Whether you are a small 15 employee organization or a large Fortune 500 company, chances are good that you face some challenges regarding this issue. Now is the time to inform, educate and provide support to your leaders, staff and customers.

You may be a Human Resource professional who has been dealing with these issues your entire career and need a refresher; you may be a leader that has left it in the hands of others to create this climate. Regardless, this book will provide you with basic knowledge and tools to assure that your employees are informed and are working in an environment they can be proud of. It's time to step up and let your managers, staff and customers know that your organization has zero tolerance for inappropriate behavior and harassment. Now is the time to demonstrate true leadership and to assure that you are creating a safe, hostile free, professional environment.

#METOO/TIME'S UP

The #METoo Movement was originally used by social activist, Tarana Burke and was recently popularized by actress, Alyssa Milano. Milano encouraged survivors of sexual assault and harassment to post #MeToo to raise awareness and to help others recognize its prevalence. In the wake of sexual misconduct allegations against Harvey Weinstein, Matt Lauer, Bill O'Reily, Donald Trump, Roy Moore, Kevin Spacey and countless others, #MeToo has spread virally on social media. Since October 2017, there have been more than 12 million #MeToo posts on Facebook, Twitter in more than 85 countries.

In January, 2018, Supreme Court Justice Ruth Bader Ginsburg, the second woman ever appointed to the high court, told her #MeToo story to an audience at the Sundance Film Festival, where a documentary about her life, **RBG**, had its world premiere. Ginsburg said that as a student at Cornell University, her chemistry instructor offered her a *"practice exam"* before an impending test. Feeling less than confident in her own aptitude in the subject, she agreed, and took the test he offered. But when it was time to take the real class exam, she found it was identical to the practice test. *"And I knew exactly what he wanted in return,"* she said.

"Every woman of my vintage knows what sexual harassment is, though we didn't have a name for it," said Ginsburg, adding that the attitude women faced was *"get past it,"* and *"boys will be boys."*

The **Time's Up Movement** got started in January 2018 with the goal of addressing inequality and injustice in the workplace by improving laws, employment contracts and corporate policies. The **Time's Up Legal Defense Fund**, administered by the National Women's Law Center, was created to defray legal costs for those who have experienced sexual harassment, discrimination, or other forms of retaliation in the workplace.

Millions of women and men are now admitting that, at some time in their lives, they have been sexually harassed or assaulted. This outcry tells us that there is a world-wide crisis that needs to be addressed. This also tells us that we are in the midst of a movement where people are speaking out against assault and harassment and will no longer keep quiet and tolerate such behavior. This tells us that it's time for organizations to take a hard look at their culture and to begin to take workplace harassment seriously.

HARASSMENT AND THE BOTTOM LINE

Harassment in the workplace has many consequences. In order to get your attention, I will begin with something that impacts all businesses - MONEY. When harassment occurs, there's a chance your organization can be sued by an employee who faced illegal workplace harassment. The repercussions of these lawsuits can be financially devastating to an organization. The costs of investigation, attorney fees, absenteeism, employee turnover, decreased performance and productivity which can lead to depression and other illness can have a significant effect on an organization's bottom line.

According to SHRM, *(Society for Human Resource Management)*, actual out-of-pocket costs for a company can range anywhere from $100,000 to millions of dollars. Of course, this number depends on the facts and complexities of a case, including whether it is litigated or settled.

In 2016 alone, there were close to 27,000 sex-based harassment claims filed with the EEOC *(Equal Employment Opportunity Commission)*. These are only federal cases; each state has additional claims filed each year. For example, in Florida in 2016 there were 7610 harassment claims filed with the FCHR *(Florida Commission on Human Relations)*. There is currently no data available for federal or state claims for 2017, but my guess is we will see a growing number of claims for 2017 and forward. Note that these are only the claims that have been filed!

And if those numbers aren't enough to scare you, think about the additional consequences of harassment. There are a variety of costs that can be even more difficult to quantify. These can include employee morale, loss of trust, goodwill, loyalty and respect. Additionally, an organization's name can be dragged through the mud having a significant impact on reputation and ultimately customer relations.

WHY EMPLOYEES SUE

I will start by saying that I am not an attorney, but I have been involved in many harassment claims during my long career. I have learned that having a clear understanding of why employees sue can be a very effective tool in preventing harassment. With all the people coming out of the woodwork, and the large number of harassment lawsuits in the system today, it's important that employers have an understanding of why an employee may decide to sue.

Motivation may vary from employee to employee. It's true, many employees may simply want a financial reward from the organization for their pain and suffering, but this is not the only reason why employees sue. Some may sue because they feel as if they have exhausted all other avenues and the harassment hasn't stopped; others may simply want an admission of wrong doing, and an apology in order to gain closure. Often victims want to prevent others from being harassed and will call for a change in company policy. And for those who have been terminated, they may simply want their jobs back. For example, former Fox News Contributor, Tamara Holder, who had filed a sexual harassment claim against Fox stated that as part of her settlement not only would she lose her position, but that she could never be hired by any Fox affiliation. In a recent interview with CNN's Brian Stelter, Holder spoke for herself and others and said, *"...there are so many women, Brian, who are hurting. We just want to work again."*

Regardless of why employees sue, lawsuits can be extremely detrimental to an organization. This book will arm organizations with the tools needed to assure that all employees are working in an environment free from harassment, and that their staff is informed, educated and trained so that these lawsuits can be avoided.

What Is Harassment?

Chapter 1

DISCRIMINATION DEFINED

Because harassment is a form of discrimination, it's important to review the definition of discrimination. We often hear people use the term discrimination when they have been mistreated or feel they have been wronged. Someone might say something like, *"I was discriminated against because I speak up and say what's on my mind and disagree with my boss."* Although that may seem like discrimination, often it is not. For discrimination to be illegal, it must be based on a "protected group" such as age, sex, or race. Title VII of the Civil Rights Act of 1964 makes it illegal to discriminate against someone on the basis of race, color, religion, national origin, or sex. The law also makes it illegal to retaliate against a person because the he or she complained about discrimination, filed a charge of discrimination, or participated in an employment discrimination investigation or lawsuit. The law also requires that employers reasonably accommodate applicants' and employees' sincerely held religious practices, unless doing so would impose an undue hardship on the operation of the employer's business.

In addition to Title VII, there are a number of discrimination laws that are designed to protect additional classes. These laws include the Equal Pay Act of 1963, Age Discrimination of 1967, Title I of the Americans with Disabilities Act of 1990, The Pregnancy Discrimination Act *(an amendment to Title VII)* and the Genetic Information Non Discrimination Act of 2009. For more information regarding these laws and types of discrimination visit www.eeoc.gov.

Although all forms of discrimination are serious and should be well understood by a company's HR team, Leadership and Management, this book will focus on one form of discrimination: **Harassment.** And because harassment is a form of discrimination, the same laws that prohibit discrimination also apply to harassment. In addition to federal laws, many states have laws that prohibit employment discrimination, including harassment. It's important that your HR team is aware of all federal and state laws.

HARASSMENT DEFINED

The EEOC defines Harassment a form of employment discrimination that violates Title VII of the Civil Rights Act of 1964, the Age Discrimination in Employment Act of 1967, (ADEA), and the Americans with Disabilities Act of 1990, (ADA). Harassment is unwelcome conduct that is a condition of continued employment or that creates an intimidating, hostile, or offensive work environment based on a perceived difference. But the conduct is illegal only if it is based on an employee's protected status. Similar to discrimination, that means that not all harassment behavior is illegal. For example, a manager yelling at an employee or a peer being rude or disrespectful may be poor behavior, but isn't necessarily illegal harassment. However, poor behavior of any kind can have a detrimental impact on an organization and should be addressed immediately.

As stated above, because harassment is a form of discrimination, the same laws that prohibit discrimination, Title VII, Civil Rights Act of 1964, ADA, also prohibit harassment. In addition, most states have additional laws that prohibit discrimination and harassment. If your organization is subject to both state and federal, it's important that your HR team and managers understand these laws. State laws can vary in many ways such as size of employees, protected status, training, etc. It's possible for employees to bring claims under both state and federal law.

TYPES OF HARASSMENT

To begin, it's important that you are aware of the types of harassment and how they can impact your organization. There are two types of harassment: **Tangible Employment Action** *(Quid Pro Quo)* and **Hostile Work Environment**.

Tangible Employment Action/Quid Pro Quo

The Supreme Court states that *"Tangible Employment Action constitutes a significant change in employment status, such as hiring, firing, failing to promote, reassignment with significantly different responsibilities, or a decision causing a significant change in benefits."*

<u>Quid Pro Quo</u> - The Ninth Circuit has held that a *"tangible employment action"* occurs when a supervisor who abuses his supervisory authority succeeds in coercing an employee to engage in sexual acts by threats of discharge or other material job-related consequence, or fails in his efforts to coerce the employee but then actually discharges her on account of her refusal to submit to his demands. Additionally, an employee can be given special treatment, promotions, preferable working

assignments, and salary increases based on the actual or implied sexual advances of the supervisor's sexual advances.

Types of Tangible Employment Action

- Firing/Hiring
- Demotion
- Failing to Promote/Promotion
- Change of Location
- Change of Responsibilities/Increased Responsibilities
- Intolerable Working Conditions

Organization's Responsibility

It is important for an employer to understand that with Tangible Employment Action, the employer is always liable for the harasser's behavior even if the organization knew about the behavior and took steps to try to prevent and correct the behavior. The organization is also liable even if it wasn't aware of the behavior even if the employee didn't report it. The organization has a legal responsibility to assure it is creating a safe, hostile free environment at all times.

Hostile Work Environment

The second, more common form of sexual harassment is when an employee is subject to a hostile work environment. The harasser does not have to be a supervisor and it does not have to be based on sex. A hostile work environment exists when an employee is subject to unwelcome conduct that unreasonably interferes with an employee's work performance and creates an intimidating, offensive, hostile environment:

- Is based on the employee's protected class.
- Is so severe or pervasive that it alters the terms and conditions of employment.
- Creates a work environment that would be hostile, intimidating or offensive to a reasonable person.

Reasonable Person Standard

In the Law of Negligence, the *reasonable person standard* is the standard of care that a reasonably prudent person would observe under a given set of circumstances. Would a reasonable person find the behavior offensive?

Unwelcome Conduct

Conduct is considered unwelcome when the employee didn't request or invite the behavior and considered the conduct to be undesirable or offensive. Conduct can also be unwelcome even if the employee submits to it or puts up with it. He/She might not report the behavior for many reasons such as fear of retaliation, causing trouble for the harasser or simply is unsure of how to handle it. Below is a list of unwelcome conduct or behavior.

UNWELCOME CONDUCT OR BEHAVIOR	
Threats	Mocking
Ridicule	Touching
Jokes	Pornography
Photos	Symbols
Pranks	Insults
Slurs, Epithets	Gossiping
Intimidation	Spreading of Rumors
Viewing Offensive Websites	Inappropriate Dress
Comments about person's body	
Disparaging Comments about person's performance	
Excluding or Isolating someone from work activity for non-work reason	
Physically blocking a person's movement or ability to work	
Texting/Emailing offensive pictures, videos or messages	
Using Social Media sites to post offensive messages, comments, or pictures	
Overly familiar relationships	

WHO CAN BE A HARASSER?

An organization is liable when it does not take reasonable steps to create a hostile free, safe environment for its employees and allows harassment to take place. The liability can vary depending on who the harasser is.

Supervisor Harassment

A supervisor can include any leader, manager, officer or employee who is or appears to be in a position to influence or change an employee's employment status. This could include anyone who has the authority or influence to hire, set pay rates, and assignments, set work responsibilities and schedules, transfer, discipline, reward, promote, suspend or terminate. Even if the harasser doesn't have the title of supervisor or manager, if the employee believes the person has the authority to do any of these things, he or she could be considered a supervisor. Additionally, if the harasser doesn't have direct authority over the employee, but has this kind of authority over other, the harasser is still considered a supervisor.

Coworker/Peer Harassment

The law views hostile work environment harassment by the victim's coworker or peer differently than that of a supervisor. However, a coworker can create a hostile work environment for a peer. If the employer ignores this behavior, or even if the victim did not report it, but the employer is aware, it will be liable. However, if an employer takes immediate reasonable steps to prevent or stop the behavior, the liability is lessened. This is why it is critical that supervisors keep a pulse on what is happening at all times. Most hostile work environment harassment can be avoided, or halted with an engaged, aware supervisor.

Non-Employee Harassment

An organization's staff often comes in contact with several people throughout the workday. Most organizations have customers, clients, patients, vendors, or other colleagues that staff have interactions with. Those people can create a hostile work environment. Organizations have the same responsibility to protect employees from harassment whether is by a supervisor, coworker or non-employee.

Who Can Be Harassed?

Often people think that harassment only exists to the person it is directed toward. This is not the case. Behavior doesn't have to be directed at a particular employee for it to be harassing. If the conduct affects an employee's working environment, it could potentially be harassment. If an employee witnesses offensive behavior toward a coworker, even if the coworker did not consider it to be harassment, the employee who witnessed the behavior may be subjected to a hostile work environment.

WHAT ISN'T HARASSMENT?

Most people spend at least one third of their day in a work environment. We all have heard stories of work romances, marriages and other relationships. Organizations don't want to create a sterile environment where people can chat, laugh and socialize. However, it's important to pay attention and have systems in place for when these relationships take place.

Consensual Relationships

Let's face it, people meet at work, date, fall in love and sometimes enter into long term relationship. It's inevitable in most environments. If a relationship between coworkers is completely consensual and there is no reporting relationship, there shouldn't be much to worry about unless there are some workplace repercussions. Sometimes dating employees' behavior can have an adverse effect on those who observe this behavior. For example, employees may demonstrate affection toward each other in the workplace or discuss intimate details about their relationship in front of others. This unprofessional behavior could lead to complaints of harassment.

Anti-Fraternization Policy - It may be tempting to adopt an anti-fraternization policy for your organization. Completely banning personal relationships may seem like an easy solution, but the reality is this is almost impossible to do and probably not the best practice. This could lead to secret relationships which can limit your knowledge and control; employees may resent it which could lead to low morale and productivity; and lastly, it may be very difficult to enforce. In most cases, the best approach to coworker relationships is not to completely prohibit them, but to discuss the parameters of professional behavior such as public displays of affection and discussing intimate details of the relationship.

Another concern an employer may have regarding consensual relationships is that often these relationships end. Often the fallout from this can have a substantial impact on those in the relationship, other employees and the organization. The separated couple may treat each other in a hostile manner affecting their own performance as well as those around them. One employee may deny that the relationship was consensual causing problems for the organization. Again, much of this may be unavoidable at times and could be tricky. Supervisors must be aware of what's happening and manage any situation that arises from it.

Relationships with Subordinates

Even though a supervisor/subordinate relationship may be considered consensual, it can cause significant problems for an employer. When one person is in a position of power, has the ability to affect aspects of the employee's employment, this could result in significant liability for the organization. It can be difficult to prevent coworkers from dating, however, it is less difficult to prohibit supervisors from dating subordinates by having a well written, well communicated policy. Additionally, given that supervisors can be personally held liable for harassment in many states, this should motivate supervisors to keep all relationships professional.

Having this type of policy will protect the organization. However, if you choose to forgo such a policy, I recommend that, at the very least, you have a policy that requires all supervisors who enter into a romantic relationship with a subordinate, report it immediately to HR. Once reported, the next step would be to separate the employees so that the supervisor no longer supervises that employee. This may create additional problems, however.

WHERE CAN ONE BE HARASSED?

So far we have discussed harassment in the workplace. It's clear that certain behavior should not be tolerated in the workplace or at work related events. However, there are also times when an employees could claim harassment even though they are not at a work event. For example, let's say that there is a company sponsored holiday party. Clearly this is a work place event and if harassment occurs, the employer may be held liable. Let's say that after the party, several employees continue the party at another location. Could the employer be held liable if something happens then? The answer is yes, it is possible. The wise decision is to investigate the situation and take any necessary action to prevent it from happening in the future.

How Can We Prevent Harassment?

Chapter 2

CULTURE AND LEADERSHIP

We hear story after story of how people have been harassed in the workplace. Some people seem to be shocked by this. I've heard senior leaders say, *"How has this happened? How is it possible this is the first I'm hearing about this?"* It's easy to point the finger and blame others. But the bottom line is that one of the primary reasons harassment exists in the workplace is because it is allowed, tolerated or ignored by leadership. Now that's not to put all the blame on leadership. Certainly, there is accountability at many levels. However, until leadership recognizes that preventing workplace harassment is a priority, it will continue at your workplace. It is the responsibility of any organization's leaders to create and support a harassment free culture. And simply having a policy in place is not enough.

Assess Current Culture

This can be one of the most difficult things that an organization can undertake. Getting a true sense of how employees feel regarding these issues is difficult. Often I'll hear leaders say, *"If it ain't broke, don't fix it."* Or, *"I don't want to open a can of worms."* I understand this sentiment; this is not an easy topic to address. It takes great courage to ask the tough questions and even more courage to accept that some of the answers may not be what you want to hear.

As part of this process, it's also important to have an understanding of how comfortable employees feel when it comes to sharing their concerns, speaking up when appropriate and reporting inappropriate behavior. Certainly there have been significant claims and we anticipate many more in the upcoming months, years, but we are still not hearing about all cases? Why? Why aren't employees reporting the incidents? Why aren't the standing up for their peers? In the Harvey Weinstein case, it was well known in Hollywood that this behavior took place. In fact, it has been written into television show scripts. At the 2013 Academy Awards, when announcing Best Supporting Actress, Seth MacFarlane joked about Weinstein, saying "Congratulations, you five ladies no longer have to pretend to be *attracted to Harvey Weinstein."* The audience laughed and cheered as if it truly was a joke and not a serious issue.

It's easy to fall into the *"this doesn't happen at our place of work"* mentality. It's easy to ignore the signs. With the current climate, this could be catastrophic. Organizations need to be preventative and proactive. They need to examine what cultural and diversity issues exist. They need to assess the culture and make plans and changes if necessary.

THE BYSTANDER EFFECT

The bystander effect is a social psychological phenomenon in which individuals are less likely to offer help to a victim when other people are present. The greater the number of bystanders, the less likely it is that any one of them will help. There are several factors that contribute to the bystander effect.

Ambiguity: the more ambiguous the situation the less likely people will intervene. If they're unclear of what's happened, they may choose to walk away.

Group Cohesiveness: People watch each other. The need to behave in correct and socially acceptable ways is important. When other observers fail to react, individuals often take this as a signal that a response is not needed or not appropriate

Diffusion of Responsibility: Often people will take *the "mind my own business mentality"* when witnesses these situations. They may feel it isn't their place to do or say something and feel it should be left in the hands of *"the boss"* or someone in power.

Fear: Often people feel they may be punished or shunned for helping others or speaking out. They can often feel intimidated and be worried about the repercussions of addressing these issues.

Sometimes harassers are protected by a culture of silence and inaction. This culture of complacency can normalize inappropriate behavior. It is the responsibility of an organization to educate, empower and encourage employees to come forward when they are aware or exposed to harassment. The days of, *"I don't want to be involved"* are over. As part of Harassment Training, many businesses are now offering Bystander Intervention Training. Through this training, employees are encouraged and empowered to become more involved in the creation of a hostile free work environment, and address and report issues. It shifts the responsibility from the victim to all who witness, or even unwillingly participate in the harassment. It sets the tone that the company will no longer tolerate any kind of harassment.

COMMIT TO REAL CHANGE

Over the years, I have been involved in working with leaders who say they want to create a harassment free environment for their employees. I've witnessed senior leaders stand up in all staff meetings or company events and passionately state that harassment of any kind will not be tolerated using phrases like zero tolerance and open-door policy. I've also witnessed them, then, retreat to their offices on *"mahogany row"* and not only ignore such behavior but, in some cases, partake in unlawful conduct.

Real change like this takes complete commitment from the most senior leaders in the organization; it takes positive role modeling; it takes visibility, involvement and support. In most organizations, any kind of harassment training begins and ends with the Human Resource team. Certainly, HR should play a huge role, but without the commitment and visibility of senior leaders, training is virtually useless. If an organization truly wants to assure that its employees work in a healthy, hostile free environment, its leaders need to be involved in policy design, training and, at times, investigations and decision making.

SUPERVISOR'S ROLE - T.I.M.E.

Having commitment and involvement from senior leaders is a great start. However, it's important to recognize that a supervisor's actions are one of the most important factors in preventing harassment. In this book the term *"supervisor"* refers to any employee that is responsible for managing, coaching and advising others – anyone who has any influence over an employee. In this section, we will discuss the role of the supervisor in creating and maintaining a harassment free culture.

Training - To begin, a supervisor needs to be well aware of the company's policy and procedures. It's critical that these supervisors receive the necessary training and education and are fully aware of their role and also their liability when it comes to harassment cases.

Involvement - Supervisors should always take harassment seriously. A supervisor's presence and awareness can dramatically decrease the number of harassment claims by addressing things before they grow. They should occasionally inspect the workplace for inappropriate items and behavior and pay attention to employee interactions. They should watch for signs of inappropriate behavior such as an employee's increased absenteeism, change in performance and productivity, withdrawal from activities and certain co-workers. Building a strong, professional relationship with employees so that they feel comfortable and safe sharing their concerns is critical. A manager's job is to listen without judgment, and to remain objective when an employee reports an incident.

Modeling Behavior – It's not enough that supervisors have training, they must then be sure that they are following the company's policies and procedures and modeling exemplary behavior at all times. They need to make the goal of respect in the workplace a top priority by creating a safe, judgment free environment allowing employees to speak up and voice their concerns.

Examine – Unless the supervisor is the person doing the harassing, chances are this is the employee's first stop. When an employee reports an incident, quite often all he/she wants is for the behavior to stop. It's critical for the supervisor to immediately take stock of the situation. Listen to the employee, examine all the evidence and take immediate action. Generally this would entail involving Human Resources or Sr. Management and moving forward with an investigation.

Do We Need a Policy?

Chapter 3

BENEFITS OF HAVING AN EFFECTIVE POLICY

All companies, large or small, should have a current, thorough policy prohibiting harassment and discrimination. An effective policy helps employees understand appropriate, and inappropriate behavior, gives them an avenue for raising concerns and complaints and shows them that the company takes complaints seriously. Additionally, in a lawsuit, an effective policy can show that the company made a good faith effort to prevent discriminatory or harassing behavior from occurring.

Good Faith Effort

Under federal law, Good Faith Effort, this means that an organization won't be held responsible for punitive damages, damages intended to punish the employer for bad behavior, even if it is found to be legally responsible for the discrimination or harassment.

ELEMENTS OF AN EFFECTIVE POLICY

The exact wording of a policy will vary from organization to organization and will depend on the organization's culture and industry. However, all effective policies will have similar elements in common.

Commitment to Preventing Harassment and Discrimination – Having a policy alone can show that you have this commitment, however, it's important that you come out directly and state it in your policy. The primary goal of a policy is to inform employees of the company's sincere intent to keep inappropriate behavior from occurring in the first place. Start with a firm, clear statement that the company does not discriminate and will not tolerate harassment or discrimination of any kind - zero tolerance policy.

Company Standard of Treatment – An effective policy should state that an employee can expect a workplace free of harassment and discrimination and that all employees are expected to act professionally and treat each other with respect at all times.

Explanation of Who the Policy Covers – A company's policy should list all applicable protected categories, such as race, gender, sexual orientation, etc. that are protected under the policy. These should include all federal and state protected categories.

Behavior in/out of Traditional Work Environment – The policy should include that discrimination and harassment are prohibited in the workplace but also outside of the workplace at company sponsored or related events, through emails and social media.

Monitoring Policy – If company monitors certain types of communication for policy violations, a company should inform employees in writing.

Description of Prohibited Behavior – In addition to including that harassment and discrimination are illegal and won't be tolerated, it should also include actual examples of prohibited behavior such as slurs, insults, comments, etc. *(See Chapter 2 for a more comprehensive list).* This will help employees understand more fully the types of conduct that is prohibited. Given how extensive the list can be, however, the policy should also state that these are examples and not an all-inclusive list.

Employment Decisions – The policy should list the types of employment decisions that cannot be based on any protected status, such as hiring, firing, layoffs, discipline, raises, promotions, work assignments or transfers.

Consequences – The policy should state that prohibited conduct will not be tolerated and can result in disciplinary action, up to and including termination.

Complaint Procedure – The policy should include how an employee may report violations, including a statement identifying the managerial employees to whom employees may report prohibited conduct, such direct supervisor, human resources, compliance officer, or senior leaders. It's important that employees have more than one avenue to voice their concerns or file complaints.

Investigation Process – The policy should include a general outline of the steps that a company will follow in response to a complaint.

Confidentiality – The policy should state that through the investigative process, the company will make every effort to disclose complaints or information only to those that need to know. However, complete confidentiality cannot be guaranteed.

Retaliation – The policy should firmly state that employees who report possible violations of the policy will not be subject to retaliation and that retaliatory conduct of any kind will not be tolerated.

COMMUNICATING THE POLICY

It is one thing to have a policy; another to communicate and make sure all employees have received, read and understand it.

New Employee Orientation – One of the easiest ways to communication the policy is during new employee orientation. Providing a new employee with a copy of the policy prior to his/her first day, gives the employee a chance to review the policy and come prepared with questions.

Acknowledgement Form – Once the employee has received, reviewed and has had an opportunity to discuss the policy, have him/her sign an acknowledgement form. This form should be put in the employee's file. This can also be done electronically through the organization's intranet system.

Yearly/Ongoing Review – Federal and State laws or regulations can change regularly. Be sure to keep your policy updated and provide updated versions to employees. Often companies will choose a date, whether it be during an annual meeting, employee review or training and provide a fresh copy of the harassment policy. A new acknowledgment form should be signed at this time. Keeping your policy updated and reviewing it with employees is part of a company's commitment to create a workplace free of discrimination and harassment.

Is Training Necessary?

Chapter 4

BENEFITS OF TRAINING

Federal law does not mandate discrimination and harassment training. Additionally, in most states, there is no law mandating training, however, it is essential that an organization, at least, consider some form of training. Training offers a number of valuable benefits.

- Establishes standards of acceptable and appropriate behavior
- Tells employees how to proceed if they have experienced or witnessed harassment or discrimination
- Reinforces the message that the company is serious about preventing and correcting violations
- Communicates the company's commitment to employees
- Bolsters the company's ability to defend itself from lawsuits
- Can help defuse the situation and alleviate stresses employees may be feeling

RESISTANCE

Some employers resist training employees because it costs time and money without an immediately apparent benefit to the business's bottom line. However, investing in training is a cost-effective preventive measure that protects both employers and employees from the greater damage.

By training supervisors, an employer prepares its frontline responders to watch for, prevent and address potential problems early and effectively. This will promote a work environment that's comfortable, functional and compliant with the law. By training employees, an employer gives everyone the information they need to meet company standards of conduct and to report any violations they observe to the appropriate managers.

SUPERVISOR VS EMPLOYEE TRAINING

Supervisors and employees can receive basic training together. However, the supervisor training will provide additional information and can either be provided separately or added to the end of a joint training. The general information can be conveyed in a joint training. This can include:

- Definitions Discrimination and Harassment Laws
- Descriptions of Protected Classes

- Company Policy
- Examples of Prohibited Behavior
- Reporting and Investigation Process
- Explanation of Retaliation

Supervisor Training

Supervisors play a critical role in preventing and managing harassment in the workplace. Generally, they are your first line of defense. Most likely, if an employee feels harassed by a coworker or leader, he/she is likely to report it to the department supervisor. Supervisors need to have a clear understanding of company policy and culture. They need to be role models, exhibiting professional behavior. Additionally supervisors may also be held personally liable for inappropriate behavior and actions. This creates a liability for individual supervisors as well as your organization.

Keep in mind that an organization can be held liable for a supervisor's actions even if the organization is unaware of the behavior. Therefore, supervisor training will include more than the basics listed above. Supervisors should also be trained on their role in supporting a harassment free culture, leading by example, discouraging inappropriate behavior, managing complaints and, in some cases, conducting investigations.

Additional Training for Supervisors can include:

- Creating a Hostile Free Environment
- Acting as a Role Model
- Responding to Complaints
- Taking Action
- Responsibility and Liability

HOW TO CONDUCT TRAINING

There are several ways to provide harassment training in the workplace. This may vary from organization to organization. Deciding who will do training will also vary. Larger organizations may use in house training professionals. Smaller organizations that don't have these resources may choose to hire a consultant.

Classroom Training – This is the most effective way to provide training to all employees. An effective training program can provide necessary information, demonstrate commitment and generate meaningful discussion. It can be tailor made to fit your organization's policy and culture and can be delivered by a combination of Human Resources, Supervisor, Leaders and/or a consultant.

Webinars – Webinars can be a useful, cost and time effective method for providing training. Webinars can be live or recorded.

You can purchase a product or you can create one of your own. If you choose to go this route, I recommend that it include an introduction from a senior leader illustrating the organization's commitment to creating a harassment free environment. A recorded webinar can also be effective as an annual refresher course.

E-Learning – E-Learning generally is a brief online session followed by a short quiz. It is not the best option as there is minimal participation and zero discussion. However, E-Learning can be used as a refresher course for those who have participated in ether a Classroom Training Session or a Webinar.

Regardless of what type of training you choose, it's critical that leadership be involved. I recommend that. at the very least, a senior leader be present for at least part, if not all, of a training session. In fact, the most successful training programs I have conducted, involved a leader being involved in the design of the program as well as conducting part of the training. This clearly sends the message that creating and maintaining a harassment free culture is critical to the success of the organization.

What Does It Mean To Investigate?

Chapter 5

How quickly you respond to a harassment complaint and the way in which you respond can be critical in affecting the outcome of a situation. It takes a great deal of courage to file a complaint and report inappropriate behavior; often it is a last resort for the employee. Generally when someone reports the behavior, the goal is simply to make it stop. The faster you respond and begin your investigation the more successful you will be in resolving the issue and protecting the organization. The longer you wait, the more liable you the organization may become. Let's walk through key steps when receiving a complaint.

RECEIVING THE COMPLAINT

There are several ways you may receive a complaint: by the accuser, co-workers, or a supervisor. You may also receive an anonymous letter or be given documentation regarding a filed lawsuit. Once you receive the complaint, you must take immediate action.

A word about confidentiality – Often when someone makes a harassment complaint, they will request that you keep the information confidential. As tempting as it is to say you'll do that, you cannot. Once this information is shared with you, you will have to investigate. This may include involving the accused employee, Human Resources and others. Let the employee know that you will do your best to keep information confidential, however, in order to resolve the issue, complete confidentiality cannot be guaranteed.

GATHERING INFORMATION

As you meet with the employee, your goal is to get as much information as possible so that you can begin your investigation. The initial discussion is key. It's important that you remain professional and respectful and that you keep your personal opinions to yourself. You've got to gain trust and you will only do this if you are empathetic, kind and non-judgmental.

Let her tell her story at her own pace, providing breaks if necessary. When she is done, be sure to ask her what she thinks should be done to resolve the issue. This will instill confidence and includes the employee in the problem solving process. In many cases, the best results come if the accuser talks to the accused on her own. Often, however, the accuser doesn't not feel comfortable doing this.

Explain the investigation process. Often this frightens an employee, and you may hear something like, *"Never mind; I don't want to proceed."* Unfortunately, this is not an option. You must respond to the issue. Reiterate to the employee that you are there to help and make things better and that you are required to investigate the complaint. This may mean discussing the issue with the accused, a supervisor and Human Resources. Lastly, assure the employee that retaliation is illegal and should be reported if it occurs.

CONDUCTING THE INVESTIGATION

As you begin to conduct your investigation be sure that you create a thorough plan which will include who, where, when all interviews will take place. It's important that you prepare any questions in advance and have a prepared initial statement. The more prepared and organized you are, the better the results. Do not drag your feet. The longer you wait, the more vulnerable the employee and the organization can be.

When the complaint involves the employee's supervisor, it's possible that you will have to separate the accuser from the supervisor as you conduct your investigation.

INTERVIEWING TIPS

BE PREPARED

EXPLAIN THE PROCESS

BE PATIENT

GET THE FACTS

LISTEN CAREFULLY

TAKE ACCURATE NOTES

REMAIN CALM, RESPECTFUL AND PROFESSIONAL

BE FAIR AND NON-JUDGMENTAL

COMPLETING YOUR INVESTIGATION

Once you have completed your interviews and gathered all your information, you'll need to come to a conclusion. This isn't always easy especially if you have spoken to many people and have varying opinions of what occurred. Keep in mind, though, that your overall goal is to determine if company policy has been violated and if there's truth to the complaint. Your job is not to determine if the law was violated. This is not always possible, however. If you've conducted a thorough investigation and have documented the investigation, you've done your job. If the behavior did occur, but there's not enough evidence, the process alone will likely discourage similar future behavior.

TAKING ACTION/COMMUNICATION

If you have determined the behavior took place, you'll need to take action. Your goal is to come up with a resolution that will prevent the behavior from reoccurring as well as disciplining the employee who conducted the behavior. This discipline will vary depending on the severity of the situation and can include anything from a written warning or training to suspension or termination. This immediate action will send the message that inappropriate behavior will not be tolerated under any circumstances.

Depending on what type of discipline you have decided to take, it's critical that you meet with the accused privately to let him/her know what you have found and what action you will take. Often the accuser will continue to deny the behavior. When possible, discuss the results and action with a witness present. Explain the results of your investigation and what discipline will take place. Be respectful and professional at all times. Remind the employee that retaliation of any kind will not be tolerated.

You'll also need to speak with the employee who filed the complaint. This can be tricky as you want to assure the employee that you have taken appropriate steps, but you do not want to divulge the details of any disciplinary action you have taken with the accused. A good way to address this is by reiterating the investigation process, let the employee know that you have come to a conclusion, and that you have taken the necessary steps to stop any future harassment. Remind the employee that retaliation of any kind should be reported.

AFTER THE INVESTIGATION

As is common in most places of business, there are very few secrets when it comes to these kinds of situation. Employees talk and this talk can lead to a number of things.

Additional Complaints – It's quite possible that once you've demonstrated that you are vigilant when dealing with such cases, additional employees may come out of the woodwork with additional complaints. If other employees come forward, be sure to address each case separately. Additionally, this information could be helpful in determining if there is a pattern of incidents or a repeat offender. Take each case seriously and take the necessary steps to address them.

Gossip – People talk and the rumor mill will get started during an investigation. It's not unusual for people to want to know what has happened and what's being done about. It's also not unusual for people to have inaccurate information and discuss it with their co-workers. When dealing with gossipers, be sure to speak with the person on a one-one basis. Tell them what you know and ask them to voice any concerns they may have. You can't stop people from talking to each other about their concerns, but you can appeal to their professionalism and answer any questions they may have. This often puts a halt to the gossip.

Do not address the organization as a whole with an all staff email or announcement. This will only frustrate those who have not gossiped and send a negative message. If you need to announce a termination or transfer, simply do so with the facts of the change. Do not include any information regarding the investigation or reasons for the change.

How Important Is Documentation?

Chapter 6

ELEMENTS OF GOOD DOCUMENTATION

Good documentation is a crucial element of any investigation and its purpose is to manage all information that relates to your investigation. These documents will be used when making important decisions. Accurate records are also helpful in protecting the organization. When you conduct an investigation, it's important to maintain several documents. These may vary depending on the type of incident and investigation. Below are key elements that may be included in your investigation file.

Names – When conducting interviews, often people will neglect to write the full name of the interviewee. Be sure your notes are clear and include full names and titles of the person. These documents may be referred to in the future, long after you or they are gone.

Dates – During some investigations, you may meet with several people. They can run into each other. Be sure you write down when you spoke to the person and be clear about any dates they refer to regarding any incidents they witness. The more factual you are, the better. It could be helpful to create a timeline of events to keep track of the interviews.

Summary of Complaint – A summary of a complaint should be simple and factual. It should state what occurred, who was involved and the date, time and place of the incident.

Interview Notes – When conducting several interviews, you may get confused and forget pertinent information. With every witness you interview, it's critical that you take notes and immediately write a summary of the meeting. Be sure the notes include the date, name, comments and, when appropriate, direct quotes.

Witness Statements – There may be times when you receive written statements from employees. This is rare and often is not the best way to receive needed information. Employee statements may be very vague and include emotion and opinion. It's better to interview an employee and write your own summary. But if you do receive these statements, they should be included in the file.

Evidence – During your investigation, a witness may provide information such as letters, emails, text messages, photographs, notes, etc. It's important to keep these in your investigation file.

Final Report – Your final report should include a summary of your investigation with any pertinent evidence and any recommendations you may have. As an organization, you should determine who the report will be shared with so that appropriate action, if needed, can be taken.

MANAGING DOCUMENTATION

It's important that you keep any information regarding the investigation safe and secure. Be sure to keep all documents in one file. Keep them separate from personnel records and be sure they are kept in a secure, locked cabinet. You may also keep them in a secure electronic file. These files should be kept for as long as you keep other important files such as employee records.

www.ingramcontent.com/pod-product-compliance
Lightning Source LLC
Chambersburg PA
CBHW030055230526
45471CB00003B/1106